MW00442113

A
DAY IN
THE LIFE
OF
**THE
BEATLES**

A
DAY IN
THE LIFE
OF
THE
BEATLES

DON McCULLIN

RIZZOLI
NEW YORK

New York · Paris · London · Milan

At first I thought that trying to create a book out of a single session would never work, but as we did so much that day, it does. For us this was a great day out.

At this point, in 1968, we were looking for something different. We were working on the 'White Album' and it was a dark period. It was a great album, but difficult to make. The word 'heavy' appeared around this time. We knew of Don McCullin from his war photography. We were all interested in photography. It was at the forefront of the culture of the time. We'd been photographed by just about everybody. We'd worked with the great photographers, with Avedon, Parkinson and Bailey. We knew how good Don was. Don's work was never 'bang-bang', but really focused on the human face. We were always looking for shots for album covers or magazines, and we thought about Don. It didn't matter that he was a war photographer. He was still a photographer.

I arrived in a pink suit and he shot some colour. We had also brought some other clothes along. We suggested some locations, and so did Don. We went to the graveyard and down to the river. We found ourselves in this hall with a piano and a parrot which was surreal, but the times were surreal.

I used to sit round at my house with Robert Fraser, the gallery owner, listening to music. I'd started talking to him about having a folly. I loved the idea of follies and he put me in touch with an English architect who came up with my geodesic dome. It was my meditation platform. The dome is still there with a little Japanese garden leading up to it. So that's where we all ended up, in the dome.

Don's a very cool guy. He is one of the great British photographers. We thought we've got to be the war. We'll provide the battlefield and it'll work. He'll just click into action. That's exactly what happened.

PAUL McCARTNEY,
May 2010

A Mad Day Out

DON McCULLIN

W e didn't know where it was all going. We just didn't know.

One day in 1968 I got a phone call, which I thought was just a joke. An unfamiliar male voice said he was phoning from Apple and wondered if I would consider spending a day photographing the Beatles for a fee of two hundred pounds. They were a little tired of approaches from photographers and wanted to get a fresh supply of pictures. They would return the negatives and I would keep the copyright.

I suppose, given the year, with all its political associations, they thought they could work with somebody who might be politically sympathetic. They didn't know that I had practically levitated a couple of inches off the ground. I would have given *them* two hundred pounds.

It was a strange Sunday. I drove in from Hertfordshire to be with the most famous group of people in the world. In a way I did it in a haze. It was quiet and they came to the *Sunday Times* building on Gray's Inn Road. At the top of the building was a photo studio that had been created by Tony Snowdon. There was no agenda except they wanted to give *Life* magazine a cover picture, which I photographed in colour. I used Ektachrome, and Ringo's chrome yellow shirt jumped out of the blue of his suit. I turned on the wind machine. It was chaotic. I'm not a studio photographer. I'm a battlefield photographer. I knew how to deal with certain kinds of photographic calamities, but not on this scale. I was slightly in awe and out of my depth. I wasn't accustomed to the speed of their world. I was used to running street battles and this was something different. These four, at the height of their power, were very different personalities. John Lennon and Paul McCartney were clearly the leaders. George Harrison was the most subdued, and Ringo appeared to step back a little. The wind machine was throwing their hair around and their famous faces looked like the figures on Mount Rushmore. To my amazement it worked and we got a beautiful cover. Thinking back on it, *Life* used to pay five hundred quid for a cover so maybe I actually lost out on it, but I was thrilled. The magazine ran a story with lots of other people's pictures. There were some truly great photographs of the Beatles before this absurd day. It is hard enough managing people one to one, but here I had four of them. I didn't have the personality or charm to deal with the situation like Bailey, Lichfield or Terence Donovan. I didn't have their backup either. I was managing on a shoestring.

We left the *Sunday Times* building and went up to a little park just north of King's Cross, then headed to the East End and Cable Street. There would have been more chaos if I had taken them to the West End. There would have been riots. I thought the East End would appeal to them, especially the river and the feeling of the docks, which they might associate with Liverpool. Also, I knew parts of Whitechapel like the back of my hand.

I immediately got a sense of John Lennon, but I didn't even realise his wife was attached to him until I got in the limo. I remember sitting with them as a family pulled up beside us in another car. They looked like they were rough from a hangover and they peered in. When they realised who was there they began clawing at the windows and waving. Lennon just waved back, cursing them as he waved.

We reached Old Street roundabout and I just asked them to get up on it. Once they were on the roundabout they obviously thought they might as well do something and performed completely spontaneously for me. You can't direct people like that. The choreography was theirs. The taxi drivers couldn't believe it as they came round and caught this free show.

We went down to the river at Limehouse, near those beautiful Georgian sea captains' houses. Lennon started stripping off, so did Paul McCartney. I suppose that meant they were relaxed. Then I took this bizarre photograph where Lennon appeared to pose as if he were dead. Maybe he was pretending to sleep, to look as if he was inebriated, but I'm convinced he was staging his own death. Again, this was 1968 and the height of the Vietnam War, from which I'd just returned. I was using my Nikon F's, which I'd brought back from the battlefield. I think everything Lennon did was a protest. Every statement he made seemed to come out of anger. There were many contradictions to him. He was a talented man who could write about peace and love, but deep down he was a forceful and aggressive. Paul McCartney was much warmer. Years later Paul asked me to photograph sad-looking women to represent Eleanor Rigby, and they were projected on a huge scale for one of his concerts.

We found ourselves in a strange community hall somewhere in the East End. Somebody produced a parrot. The light was terrible and I was struggling with reloading my cameras. There was an old upright piano and they started fooling around with it. Then we went back to Paul McCartney's house in St John's Wood, and after having tea we went out into his garden where there was this dome, like something out of James Bond or Doctor Who. We all lay around with a huge floppy dog in this strange science-fiction-like space.

I got shot of any inferiority feelings I might have had years ago, but I can never be completely comfortable photographing famous people, and you couldn't get more famous than these four. They may have been disappointed with me. I had no words of wisdom. The day was a hit-and-run accident. They just threw themselves into situations. They completely opened themselves. They gave me every opportunity, and then they took over. It was a blessing they did.

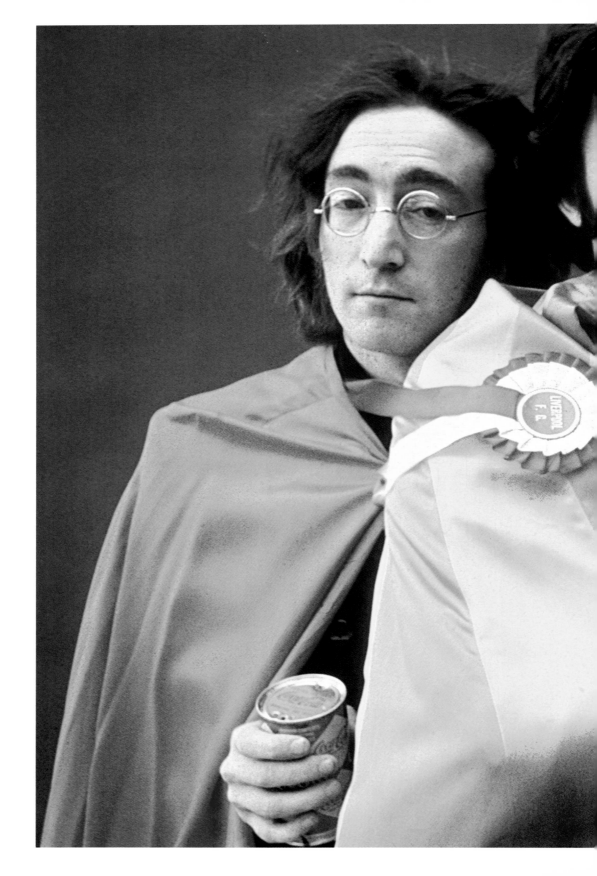

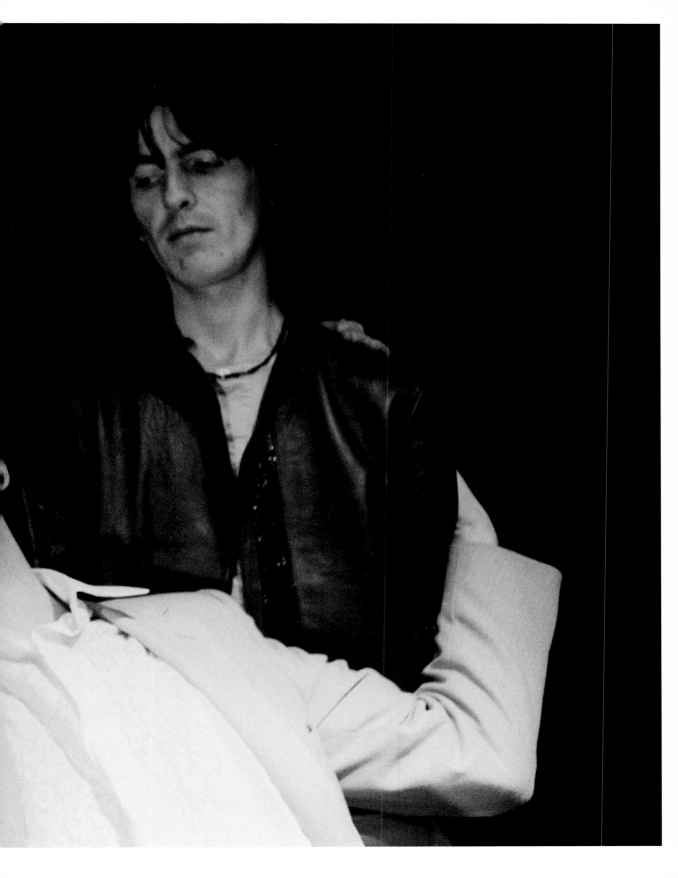

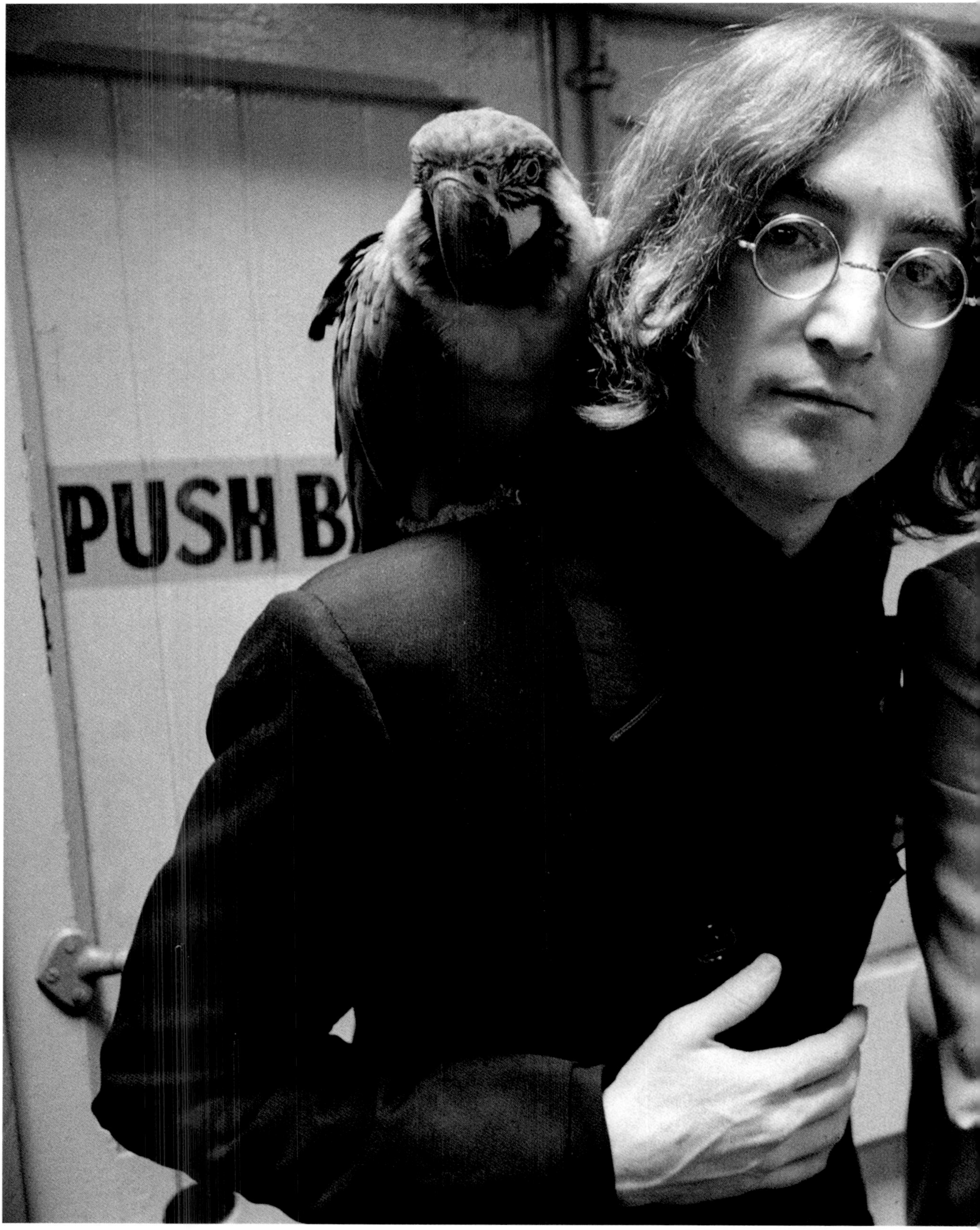
PUSH B

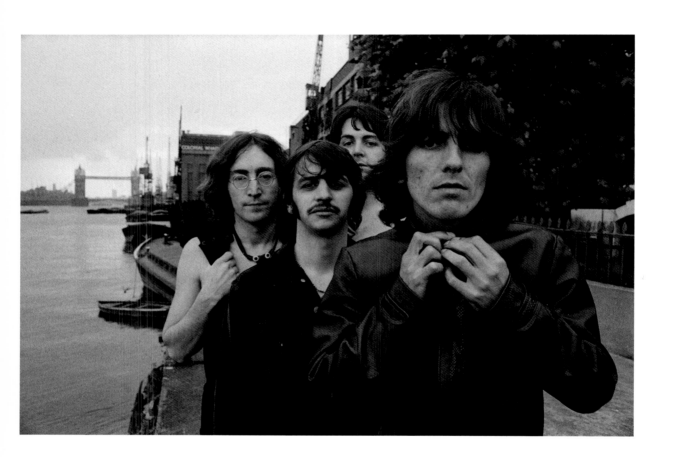

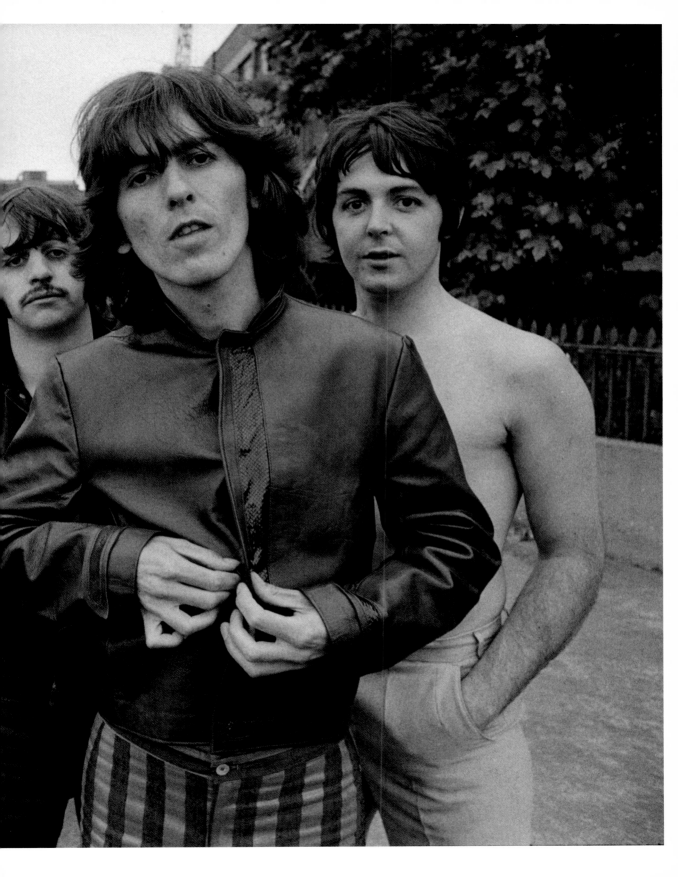

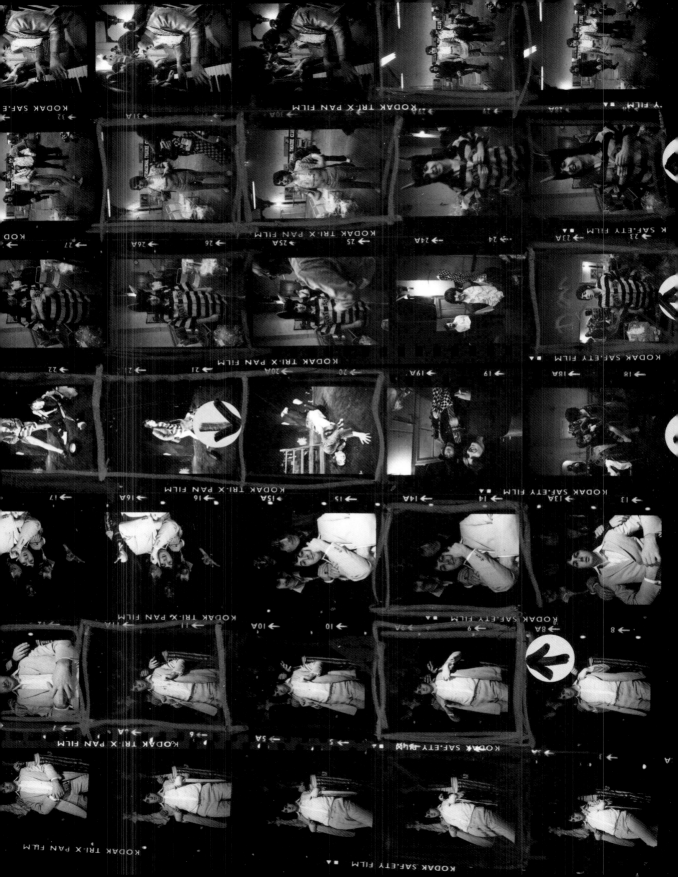

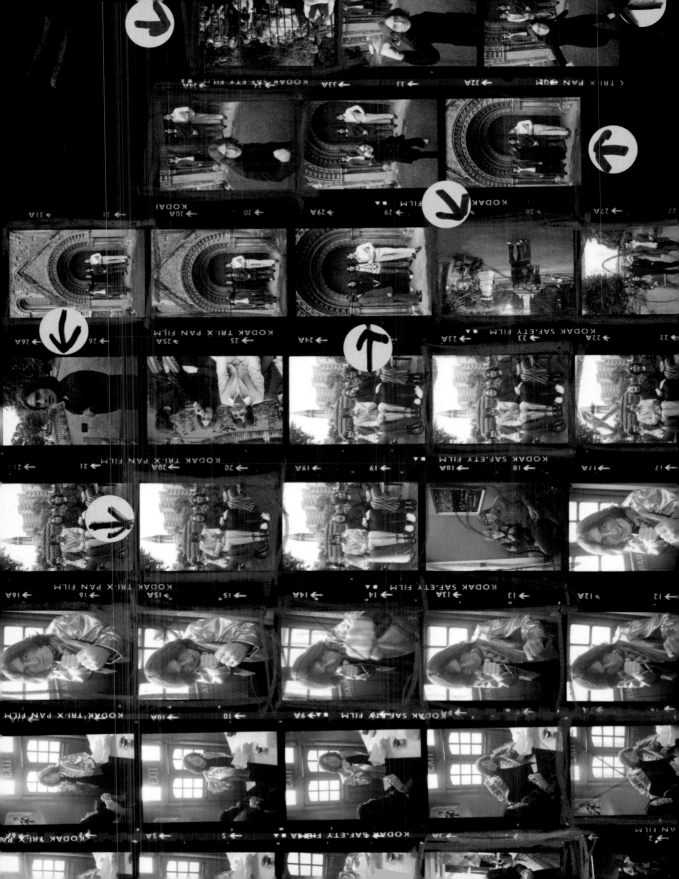

First published in the United States of America in 2010 by
Rizzoli International Publications, Inc.
300 Park Avenue South
New York, NY 10010
www.rizzoliusa.com

Originally published in Great Britain in 2010 by
Jonathan Cape
Random House
20 Vauxhall Bridge Road
London SW1V 2SA
www.rbooks.co.uk

ISBN: 978-0-8478-3611-6

Library of Congress Control Number: 2010928996

2010 2011 2012 2013 2014 / 10 9 8 7 6 5 4 3 2 1

Printed in China